What the sheep taught me

Mary Mulholland

Former journalist and psychotherapist, Mary Mulholland
currently writes and lives in London. Her poems have
been published in a wide range of journals, including
AMBIT, Perverse, Arc, Aesthetica and *Under the Radar.*
She has a Poetry MA from Newcastle University/ The
Poetry School, founded Red Door Poets, is co-editor
of *The Alchemy Spoon,* and is a founder member of the
Crocodile Collective. This is her debut pamphlet.

First Published in 2022
By Live Canon Poetry Ltd
www.livecanon.co.uk

978-1-909703-61-2

A CIP catalogue record for this book is available from the British Library.

Contents

SHEPHERDESS 5

The Call 6

Preparing for Sheep-Sitting 7

Lessons in Shepherding 8

Testing your Strength 9

The Club 10

Kiss 11

The Binding 12

The Lyrids 13

She flies alone 14

waggle dance 15

What the sheep taught me 1 16

accident of birth 17

clearing the brambles 18

demands 19

The sky holds only silence and clouds 20

drawn by fire 21

Rereading the evening 22

Ragwort and Cinnabar 23

Messages 24

Still Life 25

What the sheep taught me 2 26

journeying home 27

The Nursery of Rejects 28

Things our mothers didn't tell us 29

on the last day 30

Hymn to Sheep 31

Acknowledgements and thanks 32